SandCastle

What Should I Eat?

The Food Pyramid

Amanda Rondeau

Consulting Editor
Monica Marx, M.A./Reading Specialist

ABDO
Publishing Company

Published by SandCastle™, an imprint of ABDO Publishing Company, 4940 Viking Drive, Edina, Minnesota 55435.

Printed in the United States.

Credits
Edited by: Pam Price
Curriculum Coordinator: Nancy Tuminelly
Cover and Interior Design and Production: Mighty Media
Photo Credits: Banana Stock, Brand X Pictures, Comstock, Eyewire Images, PhotoDisc

Library of Congress Cataloging-in-Publication Data
Rondeau, Amanda, 1974-
    The food pyramid / Amanda Rondeau.
        p. cm. -- (What should I eat?)
    Includes index.
    Summary: A simple introduction to the six foods groups and and the importance of
        good nutrition.
    ISBN 1-57765-832-9
    1. Food--Juvenile literature. 2. Nutrition--Juvenile literature. [1. Food. 2. Nutrition.] I.
    Title.

TX355 .R66 2002

641.3--dc21

                                                                          2002018362

SandCastle™ books are created by a professional team of educators, reading specialists, and content developers around five essential components that include phonemic awareness, phonics, vocabulary, text comprehension, and fluency. All books are written, reviewed, and leveled for guided reading, early intervention reading, and Accelerated Reader® programs and designed for use in shared, guided, and independent reading and writing activities to support a balanced approach to literacy instruction.

Let Us Know

After reading the book, SandCastle would like you to tell us your stories about reading. What is your favorite page? Was there something hard that you needed help with? Share the ups and downs of learning to read. We want to hear from you! To get posted on the ABDO Publishing Company Web site, send us email at:

sandcastle@abdopub.com

SandCastle Level: Transitional

What is the food pyramid?

Fats & Sweets

Eat LESS

MILK Group
2–3
servings

PROTEIN Group
2–3
servings

VEGETABLE Group
3–5
servings

FRUIT Group
2–4
servings

PEANUT BUTTER

FRUIT JUICE

GRAIN Group **6–11** servings

*For suggested serving sizes, see page 23.

This is the food pyramid.

It helps us know
how to eat right.

Eating right helps us
stay healthy.

There are 6 food groups
in the pyramid.

The five main food groups are grains, fruits, vegetables, protein, and milk.

We should eat foods from each of these groups every day.

Each of these food groups gives us different vitamins and minerals.

Our bodies need many kinds of vitamins and minerals.

It is good to eat foods from all of the main food groups.

3 1833 04428 0755

The sixth food group is fats and sweets.

These foods taste good, but they are not good for us.

We should eat less of them.

Did you know candy and cookies are in the fats and sweets group?

It is okay to eat these foods for special treats.

We should not eat them all the time.

Did you know eating right gives us energy to learn?

Eating healthy foods helps us pay attention and gives our brains energy.

Did you know eating right gives us energy to play?

Our hearts and lungs need good foods to grow and stay strong.

Did you know eating right gives us energy to grow?

Our bones need food to grow stronger and bigger.

Can you think of foods in each food group?

What is your favorite food in each food group?

Index

bodies, p. 9

energy, pp. 15, 17, 19

fats, pp. 11, 13

food pyramid, pp. 3, 5

grains, p. 7

healthy, pp. 5, 15

minerals, p. 9

protein, p. 7

sweets, pp. 11, 13

vegetables, p. 7

vitamins, p. 9

Glossary

energy   the ability to work or play hard without getting tired

grain   seeds of cereal plants, like rice and wheat

protein   a substance found in all plant and animal cells

What Counts As a Serving?

Bread, Cereal, Rice, and Pasta

1 slice of bread	1 ounce of ready-to-eat cereal	½ cup of cooked cereal, rice, or pasta

Vegetable

1 cup of raw leafy vegetables	½ cup of other vegetables, cooked or chopped raw	¾ cup of vegetable juice

Fruit

1 medium apple, banana, or orange	½ cup of chopped, cooked, or canned fruit	¾ cup of fruit juice

Milk, Yogurt, and Cheese

1 cup of milk or yogurt	1½ ounces of natural cheese	2 ounces of process cheese

Meat, Poultry, Fish, Dry Beans, Eggs, and Nuts

2–3 ounces of cooked lean meat, poultry, or fish	½ cup of cooked dry beans or 1 egg counts as 1 ounce of lean meat. 2 tablespoons of peanut butter or ⅓ cup of nuts count as 1 ounce of meat.

▲▲▲▲▲▲ 23 ▲▲▲▲▲▲

About SandCastle™

A professional team of educators, reading specialists, and content developers created the SandCastle™ series to support young readers as they develop reading skills and strategies and increase their general knowledge. The SandCastle™ series has four levels that correspond to early literacy development in young children. The levels are provided to help teachers and parents select the appropriate books for young readers.

Emerging Readers
(no flags)

Beginning Readers
(1 flag)

Transitional Readers
(2 flags)

Fluent Readers
(3 flags)

These levels are meant only as a guide. All levels are subject to change.

ABDO
Publishing Company

To see a complete list of SandCastle™ books and other nonfiction titles from ABDO Publishing Company, visit **www.abdopub.com** or contact us at:

4940 Viking Drive, Edina, Minnesota 55435 • 1-800-800-1312 • fax: 1-952-831-1632